ECB - Educational Colorin

The WE CAN COLOR Series

Fun & Facts
Coloring Book

The Coolest Trucks
in the World!

Daniel Gershkovitz

Illustrations by Roksolana Tkach

Language Editing by Julia Ehrenfeld

Contact: daniel.g.books@gmail.com

TRUCKS WORLDWIDE

* The first truck was invented 135 years ago, in 1886!

* It had an engine of only 4 horsepower and its authorized payload capacity was only 3,300 pounds! Power from the engine was transmitted to the wheels via a thick leather strap, and the truck could reach a speed of only 6.5 miles per hour!

* The main part of a truck is called a cab where the driving systems and engine are located!

* Today, there are two types of cabs: the European, where the engine is located under the driver's seat, and the American, with the engine at the "nose" in front of the driver!

MONSTER TRUCKS

* The speed record of a monster truck was broken in 2020 and stands

  at 100 miles per hour!

* Monster truck wheels can be 66 inches high and weigh 900 pounds each!

* A monster truck can cost up to $250,000!

* The price of each tire on a monster truck can be over $2,500!

* A monster truck engine can produce 1,800 horsepower!!

DUMP TRUCKS

* Dump trucks have open-top containers used for transporting gravel,

sand, dirt, and earth!

* The dirt is loaded onto the truck using excavators, but it can unload

the material on its own by tipping the container!

* Some dump trucks have all-wheel drive to get better grip and traction

on the ground!

* Dozens of bridges and signs are damaged every year because drivers

forget to lower the dirt container back down and then drive them on

public roads while still tipped!

* Huge dump trucks are specially built for the mining industry! We will

meet them later!

CONTAINER TRUCKS

* The first container was invented in 1955 and completely changed the way we transport cargo around the world, because regardless of the type of load, the containers themselves are uniform in size and shape on the outside!

* The invention of containers also changed the way trucks are built and today they are usually loaded with one 40ft or two 20ft containers!

* 70% of goods in the USA are transported by truck!

* A port container crane needs 1:45 minutes to move a container from the hull of the ship onto a truck!

GARBAGE TRUCKS

* The first garbage truck was a small steam-powered truck operated

125 years ago!

* Today, garbage trucks can collect containers from the front, side, or rear!

* In order to reduce the volume of garbage, it is compressed or shredded

inside the truck's container!

* Some garbage trucks are operated by a driver only, with no additional

crew members!

* In recycling, different trucks are used for each type of material!

LOGGING TRUCKS

* The first logging truck entered service in 1913—over 100 years ago!

* Up to the invention of the logging truck, tree trunks were transported

from forests to processing plants by horses, bulls, and, in some places,

by elephants!

* Today's logging trucks can carry up to 40 tons of trees in one go!

* In order to unload the trucks at the factory, huge forklifts with extra-

long curved "teeth" are used!

SWAT TRUCKS

* SWAT (Special Weapons and Tactics) trucks are tailored to transport

the elite police forces of the United States!

* SWAT trucks are armored and can protect the fighters in the vehicle

even from shooting!

* The price of one SWAT truck can reach $300,000!

* Some SWAT trucks have turrets that open up on top for snipers or

submachine gun operators!

* Additional components on the truck are classified and known only to

the fighters!

TRUCKS IN SOUTH ASIA

* In parts of the Asian continent, trucks are decorated in particularly

  colorful ways, reminding drivers of the homes they are absent from

  during long journeys that may last for months!

* Decorations can be in the form of illustrations, glued metals, mirrors,

  and even an extension of the trunk!

* In Asia, trucks are often seen overloaded far beyond acceptable norms!

* In this region trucks often drive through narrow dirt roads bordered by

  deep cliffs!

MISSILE TRUCKS

* Missile trucks were invented to allow missile launchers high mobility,

thus avoiding being detected and hit by enemy forces!

* Missile trucks can carry multiple missile hives or one huge intercontinental

nuclear missile!

* When driving, the missile is placed horizontally on the truck in order to

maintain stability, but then it is lifted to a vertical position for launch!

* In wars, defense units deploy inflatable missile truck models to confuse

enemy pilots and satellites, causing them to waste precious ammunition!

CEMENT MIXERS

* Concrete mixers consist of a truck and a round boiler into which water, gravel, sand, and cement are poured. On the way from the factory to the construction site, the boiler turns around, preparing the concrete while on the go!

* Beyond mixing the concrete, the boiler must be kept rotating constantly. Otherwise, the concrete will harden and become useless!

* When the boiler rotates clockwise, it mixes the materials and prepares the concrete. When it rotates counterclockwise, the prepared compound comes pouring out of the boiler!

* Boiler capacity can reach 18 tons when fully loaded!

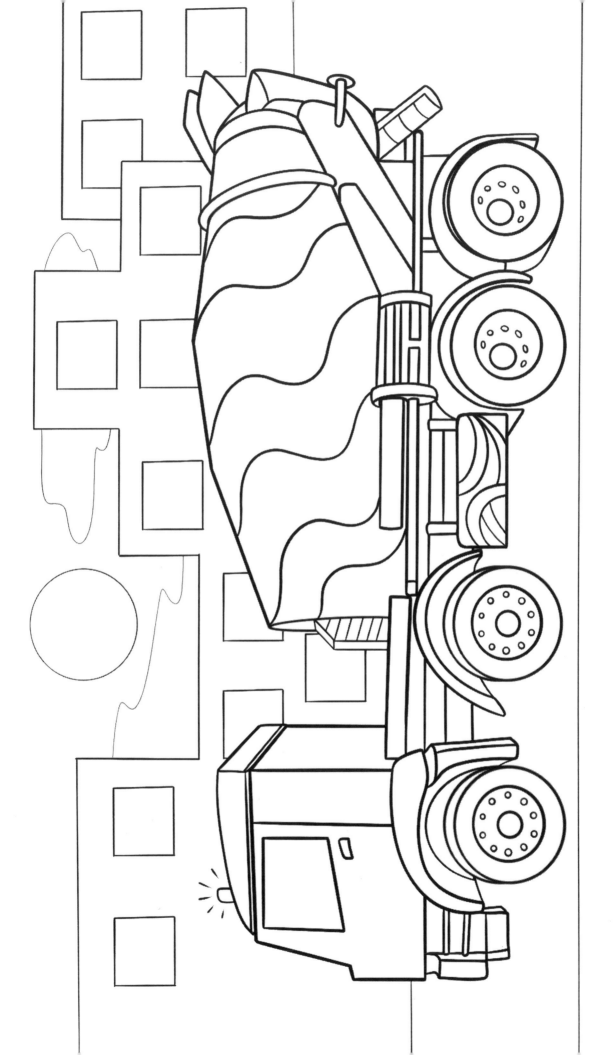

FOOD TRUCKS

* The food truck culture began at the end of the 19th century in the

   United States when cattle carriers drove their herds across the country

   and ate in carts serving them along the way!

* The first modern food truck was produced about 150 years ago!

* The US food truck market is worth $1.4 billion!

* In the past, food trucks served mostly "street food", but today you can

   find trucks serving gourmet foods fit for luxury restaurants!

TILLER TRUCKS

* The tiller truck is an extra-long fire truck carrying special equipment and ladders. It can reach a length of 50 feet!

* In order to allow these long trucks to turn in narrow streets, both front and rear wheels can be steered!

* In fact, tiller trucks have two drivers: a "regular" driver sitting in the front and a second one in charge of turning the rear wheels in the back of the truck!

* The price of a tiller truck can reach $850,000!

* In the US, it is legal for a private individual to purchase and own a fire truck!

DAKAR RALLY TRUCKS

* The Dakar Rally is considered the toughest off-road race in the world.

  Trucks weighing over 3.5 tons take part in it regularly!

* The engines of these trucks can produce 1000 horsepower!

* Apart from those participating in the race, there are other trucks that

  escort motorcycles and cars. Escort trucks are especially powerful and

  serve as a mobile repair station along the long, tough roads!

* Trucks participating in the race can reach a speed of 112 miles per hour!

HAZARDOUS MATERIAL TRUCKS

* These trucks are used to transport flammable, toxic, and even

radioactive materials!

* A special license is required to drive trucks of this kind!

* The truck's body undergoes special reinforcement to prevent damage to

the tanks in case of accidents!

* Sometimes, when it comes to particularly hazardous materials, the truck

travels late at night, when traffic is low, and is escorted by police forces

and firefighters!

MINING TRUCKS

* Dirt trucks operating in mines are the heaviest and largest trucks in

the world!

* The price of one truck can reach $3.4 million!

* The two engines of the truck produce 3,400 horsepower and are capable

of moving 400 tons of dirt at once!

* A mining truck has 6-8 wheels, each costing about $45,000!

* In order to reduce the diameter of the turn, there are trucks in which

both the front and rear wheels can turn!

ROAD RECORDS

* The longest road in the world is the 19,000-mile Pan-American Highway.

  It starts in Alaska, passes through 17 countries in total, and ends in Argentina!

* The steepest road in the world is in New Zealand—with a slope of 35 degrees!

* The widest road in the world is in Argentina and includes 9 lanes in each

  direction!

* The curviest road is in Italy with 48 twists and turns of more than 160 degrees!

* The shortest road in the world is in Scotland - its official length is only 6.5 feet!

MORE ABOUT MONSTER TRUCKS

* The longest drive by a monster truck on two rear wheels was 624 feet!

* The longest drive by a monster truck on two side wheels was 891 feet!

* The world's longest monster truck is 32 feet long!

* The height of an average monster truck is 12 feet!

* Every year, over 3,000 cars, buses, trucks, and even planes are

  destroyed in monster truck shows!

RACING TRUCKS

* The fastest truck in the world reaches a speed of 154 miles per hour!

* The most powerful truck in the world is capable of accelerating from 0 to 55 miles per hour in 4.6 seconds—faster than most sports cars!

* Race trucks are not allowed to drive on the road and therefore do not need headlights, for example!

* When trucks race, they do so with the cab only and without any cargo!!

REFRIGERATOR TRUCKS

* If it weren't for refrigerator trucks, the world would look completely

different and we wouldn't even know most of the dairy products, meat,

vegetables, and fruits we consume every day!

* The first refrigerator truck was created over 95 years ago to

transport... ice cream !

* There are over 4 million refrigerator trucks in the world!

* In order to prevent "cold escape" and energy waste, the trailer doors

of refrigerated trucks are especially thick and well insulated!

OVERSIZED TRUCKS

* Oversize trucks are used for carrying cargo in exceptional volume, weight, or size such as aircraft parts, power transformers, and even entire homes!

* There are cases where trees are felled, and signs and traffic lights are removed from the truck's way to allow it to pass through!

* In order to move a particularly heavy load, several trucks are used to pull the load together, while more trucks push it from the backside at the same time!

* When moving unusually heavy objects, a large number of wheels are needed to distribute the weight between them. The F60 Mining Machine is the largest one in the world capable of independent movement and has 760 wheels!

CONSTRUCTION TRUCKS

* The role of the road grader is to flatten the ground brought in by

bulldozers so that roads can be paved. For this purpose they use a large

blade that can reach 24 feet!

* The road roller is designed to smooth dirt and asphalt and is the last

step in paving any road in the world before it is painted!

* The weight of the drum in a road roller can reach 18 tons!

* In some parts of the world, law enforcement authorities showcase a

road roller flattening stolen cell phones and computers!

SEMI-TRAILER

* Unlike a regular truck in which the cab and cargo are inseparable, A tractor-semi-trailer is a combination of a tractor unit and one, or more, trailers to carry freight!

* A semi-trailer truck can disconnect and connect to different types of trailers on each trip. It can carry, for example, toy boxes on one trip and a water tank on another!

* To keep the driver in comfortable conditions over extra long journeys, there is a bed behind the seat, a TV, a refrigerator, a microwave oven, and other items that help them get a good night's sleep!

* Optimus Prime, the leader of the Transformers, turns into a semi-trailer!

SNOW PLOW TRUCKS

* The first snow plows were harnessed to horses as early as 228 years ago!

* Snow Plow trucks clear roads in two ways: they scrape the snow with a blade at the front, piling it aside and then, using a scattering device in the back, they sprinkle salt on the road to keep them ice-free!

* On particularly wide roads, several trucks may drive side by side to clear the snow across the entire width of the road!

* In 2014, in Pennsylvania USA, over a hundred cars crashed into one another in a pileup accident due to ice on the road!

TANK TRUCKS

* A tank truck is specially made for transporting a wide variety of liquid

  goods such as milk, wine, juice, water, diesel, gasoline, and oil!

* The first tank truck began operating in the US over 110 years ago!

* The largest tank trucks are capable of carrying 11,600 gallons of liquid,

  enough to refuel 965 cars!

* Some tanks are divided into several compartments to allow the

  transport of different types of fuels on the same trip!

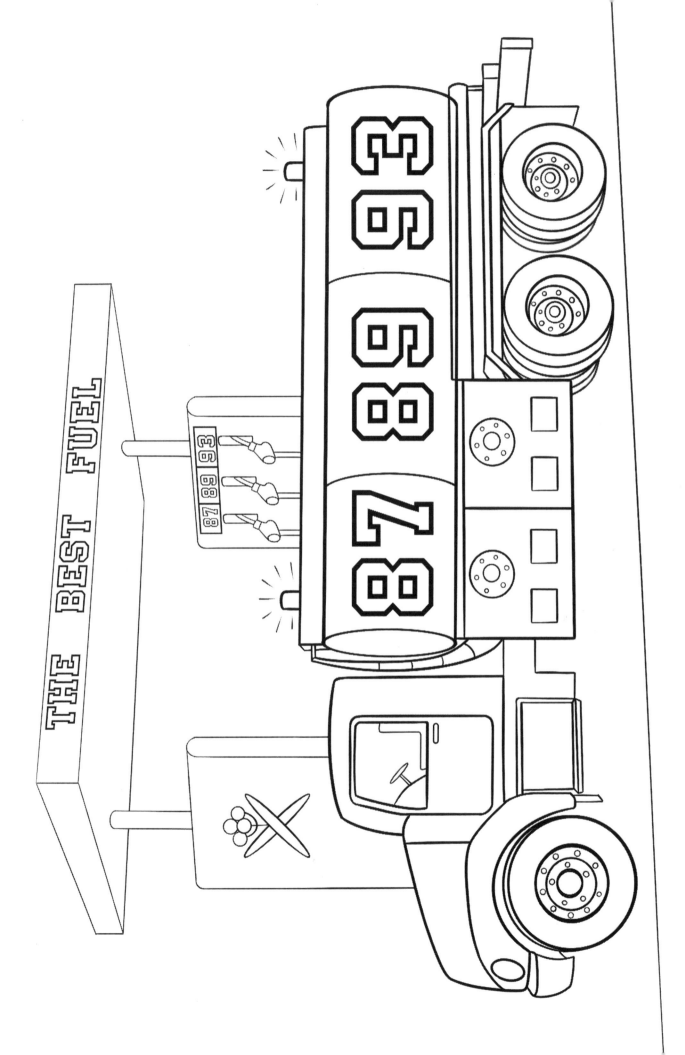

STREET SWEEPER

* The first street sweeper was actually a horse-drawn cart that moved

  alongside the workers who swept the streets in the 18th century!

* A street sweeper can brush, scrub, wash, and even vacuum dirt!

* The dirt collected is stored in a container that when full, is emptied

  into specially designated waste disposal areas!

* All cleaning operations are performed automatically without contact

  with human hands!

LIFT TRUCK

* In order to save time and money, instead of using a separate crane or forklift, many trucks are equipped with a small crane, so the truck can load and unload on its own!

* Apart from the lifting hook, there are various devices for collecting branches, stones, bulk gravel, and even a special basket to lift workers up to great heights in order to repair power lines, prune trees, hang signs, and more!

* In order to allow a good viewing angle for the operator, some cranes are operated by remote control!

* Apart from the "lift trucks" which are fitted with a large crane, there are "crane trucks" (portable cranes) used at construction sites!

ROAD TRAIN

* The Australian Desert Road on which most road trains travel, is the

only public road in the world that has no speed limit!

* Road trains are in fact huge trucks, about 160 feet long and weighing

115 tons with an average of three to five trailers attached to one cabin!

* The average number of wheels on road trains is 64!

* The longest road train in the world included 112 trailers!

SCREW-PROPELLED TRUCK

* The screw truck was developed to drive on particularly difficult terrain

such as sand, snow, swamps, and mud!

* Screw trucks have no wheels! They move atop two screw-like rollers

that push it forward!

* In order to turn, the screw truck driver locks one of the screws in place

while the other one continues to turn—the same principle as in tanks!

* Some models of screw trucks can float and sail on lakes like boats!

OPEN CRATE TRUCK

* An open crate truck is one of the world's most common trucks because

it can be loaded with almost any type of cargo as long as it does not

exceed the size of the crate!

* In Africa, open crate trucks are used to transport giraffes!

* The popular pickup is actually a scaled-down version of an open crate

truck!

* Sometimes, in the event of an accident or rollover, thousands of oranges,

cans, toys, eggs, or anything else carried by the truck are scattered

across the road!

TRACTOR-TRAILER CAR TRANSPORTER

* The largest car ship in the world can carry 8,000 cars on one trip!

* The tractor-trailer auto is designed to transport a large number of cars

  at once from seaports to distribution points!

* Today's tractor-trailer auto transporters can carry up to 12 vehicles!

* In order not to exceed the allowable length of the truck, cars are loaded

  on top of one another in two and even three decks!

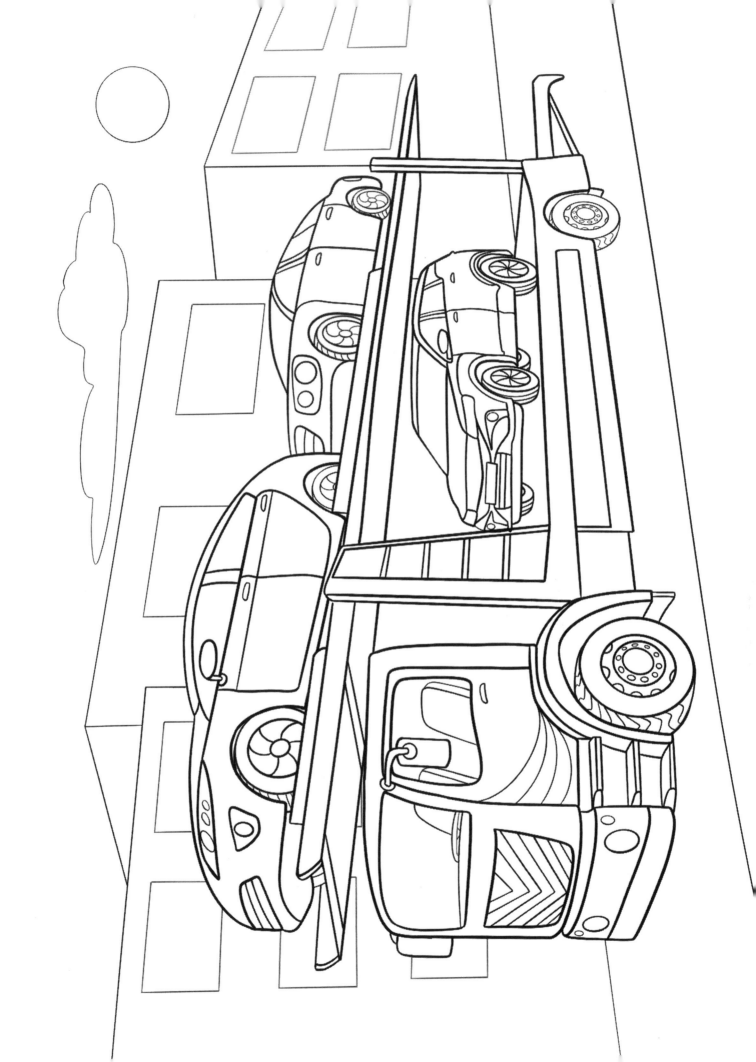

ECB

EDUCATIONAL
COLORING BOOKS

Something Smart for Everyone!

Smart, Beautiful Gifts for All Ages:

Adults, Teens, Children 3 and Up

Dear Readers,

We have made every effort to bring you the most beautiful illustrations and the coolest facts in order to give you many hours of enjoyment and enrichment of Your knowledge! As a family publishing house at the beginning of its path, your review is very important to us (hopefully, it is positive :-) and we would appreciate it if you could spend one minute of your precious time to leave a review on the Amazon site.

For your convenience, you can scan the QR code to leave your review...

For more information:
Facebook: Daniel Gershkovitz   Instagram: Daniel1980books

THANK YOU!

The WE CAN COLOR Series

Fun & Facts

Cool and Educational Coloring Books!

930 Illustrations

Scan me for more information...

Over 3,875 Cool Facts!

A WORLD OF KNOWLEDGE AND ENJOYMENT FOR ALL AGES

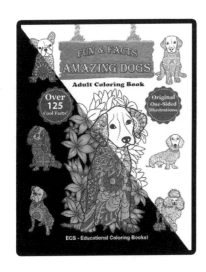

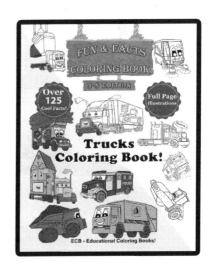

Coloring Books for Adults and Teens!

Coloring Books for Ages 5-100!

Coloring Books for Ages 3-6!

FUN & FACTS COLORING BOOKS
Amazing coloring books for teens and adults!

The perfect gift for yourself and for any animal lover with a passion for coloring detailed illustrations while enriching their knowledge!

These coloring books, for teens and adults alike, were created by the best artists and feature the most popular animals in the world in spectacular designs.

Next to each illustration you will find fascinating, funny, educational and surprising facts about your favorite dog, horse or cat - over 125 cool facts throughout each book!

All illustrations in the books are unique! There is no page that repeats itself and in order to diversify even more, we have combined in the books different illustration styles in the animals and backgrounds that include mandalas, flowers, landscape and much more!

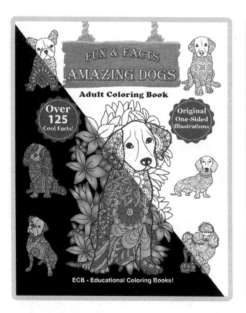

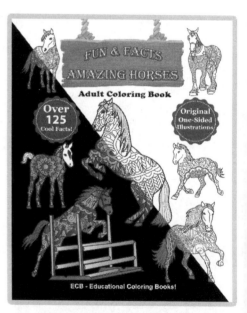

Fun & Facts
Cool and Educational Coloring Books!

22 coloring books on a variety of educational topics that will interest every boy and girl, from the age 5 to 100!

All illustrations are original, realistic and illustrated on a single side.

Over 125 educational, cool and interesting facts about every animal, vehicle, aircraft or planet that appear in one of the books!

A smart gift for a birthdays and holidays for many hours of fun, relaxation and learning!

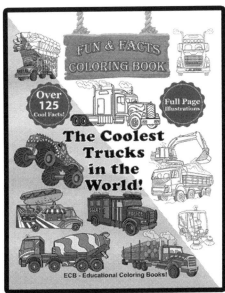

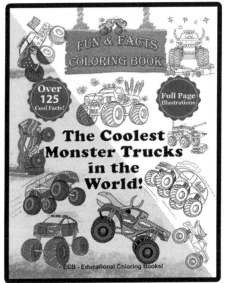

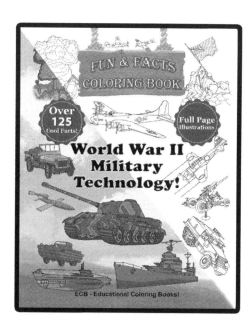

FUN & FACTS COLORING BOOK

Over 125 Cool Facts! · Full Page Illustrations

World War II Military Technology!

ECB - Educational Coloring Books!

FUN & FACTS COLORING BOOK

Over 125 Cool Facts! · Full Page Illustrations

The Coolest Airplanes of WWII!

ECB - Educational Coloring Books!

FUN & FACTS COLORING BOOK

Over 125 Cool Facts! · Full Page Illustrations

The Coolest Vehicles in the World!

ECB - Educational Coloring Books!

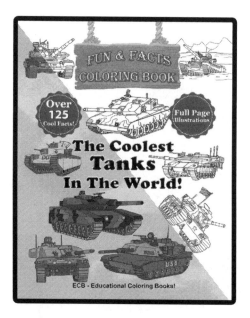

FUN & FACTS COLORING BOOK

Over 125 Cool Facts! · Full Page Illustrations

The Coolest Tanks In The World!

ECB - Educational Coloring Books!

FUN & FACTS COLORING BOOK

Over 125 Cool Facts! · Full Page Illustrations

The Coolest Construction Trucks!

ECB - Educational Coloring Books!

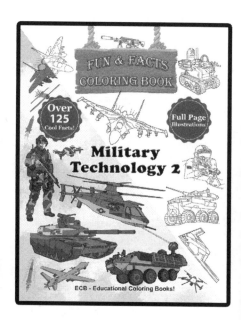

FUN & FACTS COLORING BOOK

Over 125 Cool Facts! · Full Page Illustrations

Military Technology 2

ECB - Educational Coloring Books!

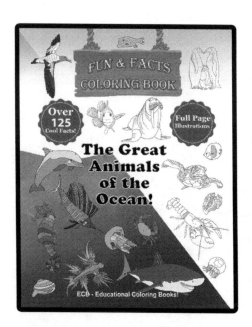

FUN & FACTS COLORING BOOK

Over 125 Cool Facts! · Full Page Illustrations

The Great Animals of the Ocean!

ECB - Educational Coloring Books!

FUN & FACTS COLORING BOOK

Over 125 Cool Facts! · Full Page Illustrations

The Great Animals of the Jungle!

ECB - Educational Coloring Books!

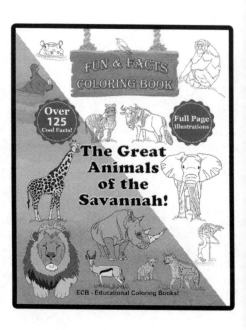

FUN & FACTS COLORING BOOK

Over 125 Cool Facts! · Full Page Illustrations

The Great Animals of the Savannah!

ECB - Educational Coloring Books!

FUN & FACTS COLORING BOOK

Over 125 Cool Facts!

Full Page Illustrations

The Great Animals of the Forest!

ECB - Educational Coloring Books!

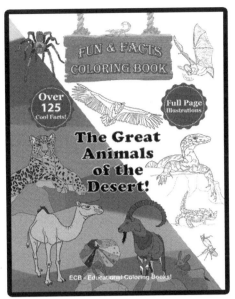

FUN & FACTS COLORING BOOK

Over 125 Cool Facts!

Full Page Illustrations

The Great Animals of the Desert!

ECB - Educational Coloring Books!

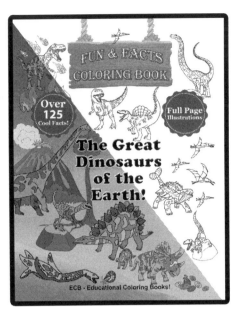

FUN & FACTS COLORING BOOK

Over 125 Cool Facts!

Full Page Illustrations

The Great Dinosaurs of the Earth!

ECB - Educational Coloring Books!

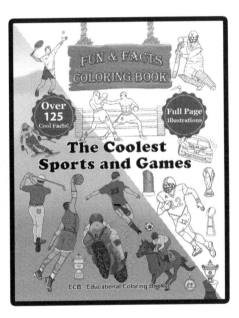

FUN & FACTS COLORING BOOK

Over 125 Cool Facts!

Full Page Illustrations

The Coolest Sports and Games

ECB - Educational Coloring Books!

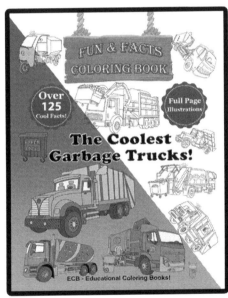

FUN & FACTS COLORING BOOK

Over 125 Cool Facts!

Full Page Illustrations

The Coolest Garbage Trucks!

ECB - Educational Coloring Books!

FUN & FACTS COLORING BOOK

Over 125 Cool Facts!

Full Page Illustrations

The Coolest Airplanes!

ECB - Educational Coloring Books!

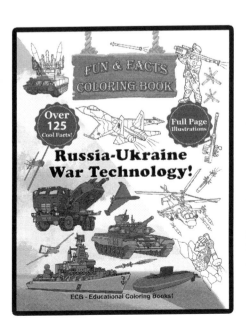

FUN & FACTS COLORING BOOK

Over 125 Cool Facts!

Full Page Illustrations

Russia-Ukraine War Technology!

ECB - Educational Coloring Books!

FUN & FACTS COLORING BOOK

Over 125 Cool Facts!

Full Page Illustrations

Powerful Trucks!
Coloring Book

ECB - Educational Coloring Books!

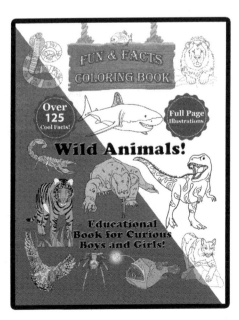

FUN & FACTS COLORING BOOK

Over 125 Cool Facts!

Full Page Illustrations

Wild Animals!

Educational Book for Curious Boys and Girls!

WE CAN COLOR
Fun & Facts
Ages 3-6 Edition

Following the success of the educational coloring books for ages 5 and up, we are proud to bring you a special and adapted edition in terms of illustrations and facts for ages 3-6!

All illustrations and facts have been designed for young children.

Over 125 educational, cool and interesting facts about every animal, vehicle, aircraft or planet that appear in each of the books!

A smart gift for birthday and holidays for many hours of fun, relaxation and learning!

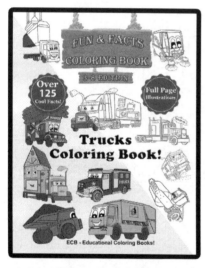

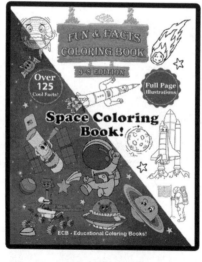

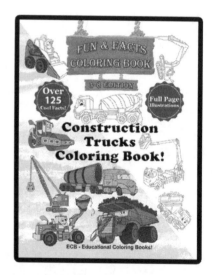

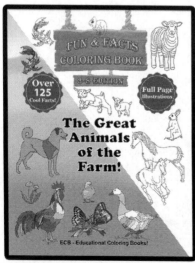

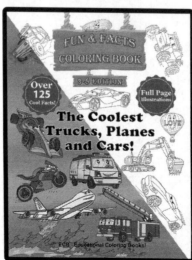

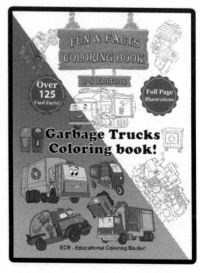

Love Facts?
This is for you!

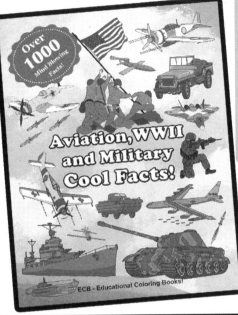

eBook & Paperback

The perfect gift for every girl for many hours of fun while coloring spectacular illustrations that will help build self-confidence, self-esteem, imagination and creativity while enriching knowledge with amazing facts on a variety of subjects!

COME WITH US ON ANOTHER JOURNEY OF FUN, COLORING AND KNOWLEDGE ENRICHMENT!

Made in United States
Orlando, FL
11 December 2024

55398904R00039